KU-065-395

THE LAST *COMPLETE IRISH GAG BOOK

A Star Original

Garry Chambers was born on April 2nd, one day too late to qualify for honorary Irish citizenship. To overcome this handicap he turned to writing scripts for such TV shows as *The Two Ronnies*, *The Bob Hope Show*, *Who Do You Do? Bruce's Big Night* and *The David Frost Show*.

'The greatest thing since sliced milk'
The Dublin Book Annual (Midday Edition)

*Almost

Also by Garry Chambers in Star

THE *COMPLETE IRISH GAG BOOK
THE SECOND *COMPLETE IRISH GAG BOOK

*Almost

THE
LAST *COMPLETE
IRISH GAG BOOK

Compiled by Garry Chambers
Illustrated by Bill Tidy

*Almost

Star

A STAR BOOK

published by
the Paperback Division of
W. H. ALLEN & Co. Ltd

A Star Book
Published in 1981
by the Paperback Division of
W. H. Allen & Co. Ltd
A Howard and Wyndham Company
44 Hill Street, London W1X 8LB

Copyright © Garry Chambers, 1981
Illustrations copyright © Bill Tidy, 1981

Printed in Great Britain by
Hunt Barnard Printing Ltd., Aylesbury, Bucks.

ISBN 0 352 30679 3

This book is sold subject to the condition that it shall
not, by way of trade or otherwise, be lent,
re-sold, hired out or otherwise circulated without the
publisher's prior consent in any form of
binding or cover other than that in which it is published
and without a similar condition including this
condition being imposed on the subsequent purchaser.

My thanks to Peter Vincent and
Rosemary Hewett for their contributions.
Special thanks to Jenny Brassett for
her help in preparing the manuscript.

THE IRISH AT HOME

Mrs Murphy is such a sloppy housekeeper, it wasn't until Murphy wiped the dust off the front of the radio that he found out it was a TV set.

Murphy told his wife he found black underwear very sexy. So his missus stopped washing his Y-Fronts.

Murphy wanted to keep an accurate record of his son's height. So, every six months, he'd stand the lad up against the wall, take a piece of chalk and make a mark . . . on the kid's head.

'Ugh, Maureen, this suet pudding you cooked is disgusting!'
'Don't be so ignorant, Sean. The recipe book says it's delicious!'

Murphy is a model husband. Unfortunately, he's not a working model.

Favourite Halloween party game in Ireland: Bobbing for french fries.

Murphy is such a phoney, as a baby he was breastfed Marvel.

Mrs Kelly has so many children that she's run out of names . . . to call her husband.

While Murphy was growing up he was one of sixteen kids, all of whom shared the same bed. In fact, he never slept alone until he was married.

How to bake a cake: make two cakes ⁄ a large one and a small one – and put both in the oven. When the small one is burned, the large one is done.

Mrs Murphy's cooking is so bad that when she goes on a diet, she *gains* weight.

Sean and Maureen feed their baby garlic so they can find the kid in the dark.

Murphy goes to bed with a tape measure to see how long he sleeps.

Murphy got home so late from work that his dinner went flat.

Maureen is a lousy cook. Her toast has to be scraped to be believed.

Old Muldoon died on the day he reached 100. It seems his friends gave him a surprise party and the shock killed him.

Sean and Maureen moved into the top floor of a 25-storey block of flats. Throughout their first week of residence Maureen was nowhere to be seen. Eventually, she turned up in a state of complete exhaustion.

'And where the hell have you been?' asked Sean.

'Oh,' came the reply, 'I've been washing the steps.'

Murphy had a very unhappy childhood. His parents were very much in love and took it out on him.

Maureen's armpits have split ends.

What causes most fires in Irish kitchens?
Housewives tossing pancake flambes.

'Hey, Maureen, some of the lads were talking down at the site today and they said that our milkman has had it off with every woman in our street except one.'
'Well, it must be that snobbish Mrs Murray at Number 26.'

Murphy thinks his missus is so beautiful that he gets drunk every night so he can see two of her.

'What's for tea, Maureen?'
'Tongue.'
'Tongue? Ugh, I couldn't eat anything that's been in an animal's mouth. Boil me an egg instead.'

Then there was the wealthy Irish bachelor who advertised for a daily woman and hired all 365 of them.

Theresa gave birth to six piglets. Now her dad is looking for the swine who did it.

When Sean is late home from the building site, Maureen keeps his dinner warm by smothering it with mustard.

Murphy's insomnia is so bad that the sheep are striking for shorter hours.

'Did you hear about Mulligan? Came home early from work last night, found his missus in bed with Casey, grabbed a gun and shot 'em both.'

'Look on the bright side, it could've been worse.'

'What do you mean it could've been worse?'

'Well, if Mulligan had come home early the night before, I'd be dead by now.'

Murphy is the dimmest man in Dublin. To give you some idea how dim he is, he thinks he lives in Tipperary.

Before sitting down to write a letter, Murphy locked the front and back doors in case his pen ran out.

Murphy's entire family are good singers. They have to be, there's no lock on their lavatory door.

BEDTIME

'Sean, set the alarm for eight.'

'But why, Maureen, there's only the two of us?'

'Oh, Sean, the laundry came back today.'
'It did?'
'Yes, that's the third time they've refused it this week.'

Murphy took an overdose of senna pods and his condition is 'touch and go'. He only has to touch something and he has to go.

'Mam, now I'm fourteen, can I wear a bra?'
'Certainly not, Joseph!'

Sean came home early from work one day and found his missus in bed with a city gent. Grabbing the toff's umbrella, Murphy broke it over his knee and sneered, 'There! I hope it rains!'

Maureen's complexion is like peaches and cream.
Yellow and fuzzy.

Maureen is so thin that she has to wear braces to keep her girdle up.

Mrs Kelly's new curtains were too short but she solved the problem by cutting six inches off the top and sewing it on the bottom.

Mrs Clancy has twenty-four children and is having another because she'd hate the youngest one to be spoiled.

Maureen has worn the same dress for so long that it's been in fashion three times.

Murphy led a very sheltered life. In fact, he was eighteen before he was allowed to look at a naked light.

VISITOR AT THE FRONT DOOR

'Good morning, sir. Can I interest you in a life insurance policy?'
'Hell, no. I've got enough life insurance to last me a lifetime.'

Murphy is such a loser, as a baby his foster parents tried to get him adopted.

'Sean, I understand you haven't spoken to your wife in six weeks?'
'That's true, Tim. I don't want to interrupt her!'

Murphy trained his dog to count and now it does Number One and Number Two on the carpet.

Did you hear about the Irishman who received a recorded delivery letter and went crazy trying to play it on his stereo?

Murphy and his missus moved next door to a pawnshop so's she'd be near her wedding ring.

Murphy can't work because of his chest. He's lost the key to it and his pick and shovel are inside.

Murphy is so thin, when the door opens and nothing comes in, it's Murphy.

In a drunken rage, Murphy attacked his wife with a razor. Fortunately, he forgot to plug it in.

It's not that Mrs Murphy is a lousy cook, but who else makes soup on a barbecue spit?

As a child, Murphy used to wet the bed. From the top of the wardrobe.

'Oh, Maureen, my Tim is one in a million. He doesn't smoke, drink or go out with women. Including me.'

Then there was the tragic case of the Irish family who lived in a ground floor flat in a high rise block. They were stranded indoors for a week when the lift broke down.

Hannigan the hippy was smoking some shit when the toilet seat slammed down on his head.

Murphy wondered why his wife was always drunk when she did the laundry. Then he discovered she was putting whiskey in her steam iron.

'Hey, Sean, which are your best socks?'

'Those over there, Maureen. The ones with the smallest holes.'

Murphy had so much trouble getting *The Irish Times* regularly that he changed his fishmonger.

Murphy recalled the nicest thing about his childhood was when the chimney sweep called and Murphy and his brothers and sisters would crowd around the fireplace and wait for the sweep's brush to come out at the bottom of the chimney.

Did you hear about the Irish housewife whose chip pan caught fire? She sucked up the flames with her vacuum cleaner.

Grogan's doctor gave him a box of slimming pills. Unfortunately, Grogan couldn't read the instructions so he took the lot all at once and lost so much weight he died. To give you some idea of how much weight he actually lost – he was buried in the empty pill box.

Irish milk bottles are made of magnifying glass to make the milk look bigger.

'Oh, Sean, I've not been myself lately.'

'Yes, Maureen, I've noticed the improvement.'

'I thought we were having a turkey.'
'No, it got better.'

Murphy was showing his girlfriend his new house. Opening an interior door, he ushered her into a room piled high with crates of Guinness.

'And this,' he announced proudly, 'is the living room!'

'Living room?' queried the bemused girl. 'This is a living room?'

Retorted Murphy, 'Well, if that's not living, I don't know what is!'

Murphy led a very sheltered life. In fact, he was eighteen before his mother would let him read the women's side of a laundry list.

Murphy suffers from claustrophobia. Whenever he's in a confined space he breaks out in a cold snot.

Maureen watched a heart operation on *Your Life In Their Hands* and felt so sick that she had to turn the sound off.

Then there's Irish ice cream. It melts in the fridge, not in your mouth.

When he was a kid, Murphy and his ten brothers all slept in the same bed. He'd come home very late so he could sleep on top.

Maureen: But, Sean, if you wanted to go to the pub, why didn't you ask me first?
Sean: Because I wanted to go to the pub!

LETTER FROM HOME

Address: Here
Date: Today

Dear son

Thank you for the Mother's Day card.

To save you looking down at the bottom of this letter to see who wrote it, it's your Mum.

Here's the latest news from home.

Your elder brother has gone to art school to learn how to become an inferior decorator.

Your cousin Sally has had a baby out of wedlock. Though personally, I don't believe in those mail order firms.

Your Uncle Frank has invited me to a Christmas Eve party but has neglected to tell me when it is.

Remember Old McKinley who is in the lunatic asylum? Well, his son Old McKinley Jr. has now been committed to the same place. If that isn't blatant nepotism, I don't know what is.

Excuse me, there is someone at the door, so talk to yourself for a few minutes while I go and answer it.

It's all right, I'm back. It was some peddlar trying to sell me some brushes. I told him I'm not as gullible as I look.

Oh, by the way, your Aunty Bridget does not have varicose veins after all. It turned out that her fountain pen was leaking.

The doctor prescribed things called suppositories for my piles, but as there were no instructions on the box, I phoned him at three o'clock in the morning and he told me what to do with them.

Remember Constable Fitzpatrick? Well, he left the

police force and has now been ordained a priest. He's already taking signed confessions.

I am sending you a dozen brushes for your birthday.

I will end this letter now or I will not have room on the page for the PS.

Your loving Mother.

PS. I will not write on the other side of the page as it would make the letter too heavy for the 14p stamp.

THE IRISH AT WORK

'How many "A" Levels have you got?'
'Three. Maths and Advanced Maths.'

It was 11 a.m. on the building site and the Foreman handed Murphy a fiver, saying, 'Go and get me and Paddy a ham sandwich each and get something for yourself.'

So off went Murphy and returned ten minutes later, handing two sandwiches to the Foreman.

'Hey, wait a minute,' exclaimed his boss, 'where's my change?'

Retorted Murphy, 'There's no change. You told me to get something for myself, so I bought a pair of longjohns.'

Dr Davis walked into the men's ward in time to see Nurse Riley leaving a screaming patient's bed carrying a huge bowl of steaming hot water. 'No, no, nurse,' exclaimed the doctor, 'I told you to prick his boil!'

Then there was the Irish baker who sold doughnuts to midgets as lavatory seats.

Murphy went into the brothel business. Nothing fancy, just his wife and her mother.

It was the Irish bingo caller's first game. He picked a ball, looked at it and announced, 'Sherwood Forest!'

Queried a woman, 'What do you mean – "Sherwood Forest"?'

Came the reply, 'All the t'rees.'

Motto of Irish opinion poll researchers: Don't talk to strangers.

Slogan of a Dublin private sewage company: Your sewage is our bread and butter.

MOTOR ACCESSORIES SHOP

'I want a car battery.'
'Rechargable?'
'Not likely. I'm only going to pay for it once.'

WATER RATES OFFICE

'I got my water bill this morning and it has a £5 charge on it for sewage.'
'So?'
'Well, you didn't deliver any sewage.'
'Ah, we tried to. But you were out.'
'Then why didn't you put it through the letter box?'

BUILDING SITE

'Sorry I'm late, foreman, but I had car trouble.'
'I didn't know you had a car?'
'I don't. That's the trouble!'

Then there's the Irish carpenter who puts the door up first and builds the frame around it.

Then there was the Irish toilet attendant who went into business for himself.

'Boss, can I have next week off to have my appendix out?'

'Okay, but don't make a habit of it.'

Father O'Field of the Church of Saint Patrick And All And All Angels is so religious that he wears stained glass contact lenses.

BUILDING SITE

'Have you finished your lunch, Murphy?'
'Indeed I have. Every drop.'

The Irish silicon chip factory is so busy, they've had to take on less staff.

Irish Judge: My court in Dublin is the one place in Ireland where justice is truly dispensed with.

Mr and Mrs Murphy have so many children that it wasn't until they had to fill in a census form they realised that two of their sons had the same name.

Murphy applied to join the Royal Navy as a deckhand on a submarine.

Police homicide photographer taking photo of corpse: Smile!

Dublin traffic sign: Drive carefully. Especially on pavements.

Boss: Hey, Murphy, would you mind showing me a little respect.
Murphy: But, Boss, I show you as little respect as possible.

PSYCHIATRIST'S OFFICE

'Now, Mrs Kelly, what seems to be the trouble?'
'Well, Doctor, I feel so unhappy because I'm so ugly.'
'Nonsense. Let's discuss it. Lie down on the couch.'
'All right . . . Like this, Doctor?'
'No, no, Mrs Kelly. Face *downwards,* please!'

JOB CENTRE

'This job pays £5,000 per annum.'
'How much is that a year?'

Murphy started a job as a furniture salesman. First day on the job he sold three items. The Manager's desk and two of his office chairs.

Irish monk: I've just taken my vow of silence and can't wait to tell all my friends.

Then there was the Irish judge who sentenced a cat burglar to life. Nine times.

Doctor to patient: I'm giving you these four pills. Take two before you go to bed and the other two if you wake up in the morning.

PHONE CALL TO A GARAGE

'I've just driven my car into a tree.'
'What make is it?'
'Ford Concertina.'
'You mean Ford *Cortina.*'
'You wait till you see it.'

DUBLIN CHEMIST SHOP

'I want a comb.'
'Steel one?'
'No, I'll pay for it.'

Irish secretary to boss: After I've typed your letter I'll type the carbon copy and then go to lunch.

Then there was the Irish obstetrician who asked the mother-to-be in labour, 'Whereabouts does it hurt?'

Murphy was on the dole for so long that the Labour Exchange presented him with a bone idol.

Irish sergeant major drilling soldiers: Left, left, left, right, right, left, left, right, left, left, right, right, right, right . . .

English customer to Irish barber: How long have you been cutting hair? I know you only started this morning, but at what time?

DUBLIN POST OFFICE

'What's that there in the corner?'
'A mail bag.'
'My God, how can you tell the difference?'

DUBLIN BARBER SHOP

'I want you to cut my hair short at the back, long on the left side and close-cropped on the right side. Then, wash my hair and get shampoo in my eyes and all down my neck and back. Afterwards, I want you to shave me, cut my chin three times and slice a piece out of my ear.'
'But, sir, I can't do that to you.'
'Why not? You did it last time!'

Then there was the Irish diplomat who was invited to an official function at the Zimbabwe Embassy to meet that country's new President. However, the diplomat couldn't remember Mugabe's name so he called him Smith.

Notice in Dublin Labour Exchange: Grave diggers wanted for sea burials. Good pension scheme.

IRISH CONVENT

'Oh, Mother Superior, this inflation is getting worse. The other day I paid twenty-five pence for a banana and could only use it twice.'

Murphy started his new job as a dustman. He lifted the lid of his first dustbin and exclaimed, 'Glory be! Someone's beaten me to it. It's already full!'

The highly sociable Murphy quit his new job as a morgue attendant because, as he said, 'Nobody would speak to me.'

'Hey, Tim, lend me a pound till payday.'
'Okay, but when's payday?'
'How should I know? You're the one who's working!'

PERSONNEL OFFICE

'I'll pay you what you're worth, Murphy.'
'Oh no, I could never live on that kind of money.'

Irish auctioneer: What am I bid for this priceless vase? Do I hear £5? Thank you, sir . . . Do I hear £4.50? Thank you, sir . . . Do I hear £4? Thank you, sir . . . Do I hear £3.50? Thank you, sir . . . Any advance on £3 . . . ? Going once, going twice . . . Thank you, sir. Gone! Sold to that lady for a pound!

Then there was the Irishman who committed suicide by jumping into a Xerox duplicating machine. Police found eighty copies of his body all over the floor.

JOB CENTRE

Clerk: Name?
Murphy: Seamus Murphy
Clerk: Address?
Murphy: 40 Abbots Road, Camden Town.
Clerk: Height?
Murphy: Oh, it must be about thirty feet from ground to roof.

Did you hear about the Irish businessman who opened a kipper factory in a smokeless zone?

Pub landlord: That new urinal I've just had installed may have cost me a fortune, but in time it'll be worth every penny spent on it.

JOB CENTRE

'Tell me, do you have a criminal record?'
'Oh no, sir. In fact, I don't even have a criminal record player.'

DUBLIN OFFICE

Typist: Excuse me, sir, but can I use your dictaphone?
Boss: No! Use your finger, same as the rest of us!

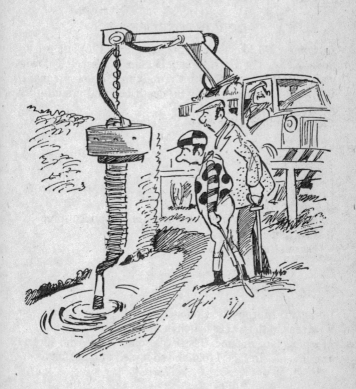

Then there was the Irish racehorse trainer who believed horseshoes were so lucky that he nailed a dozen of them on to each hoof of every one of his mounts.

Postman Pat says he'd finish his deliveries in half the time if he didn't have to make all those stops.

DUBLIN POST OFFICE

Customer: I'd like to send this telegram. I'll dictate it to you. 'Kelly, 114 Cork Street, Dublin. Father fell downstairs, mother ran off with the milkman, sister pregnant, brother in a coma, granny on death bed and grandfather arrested for rape.'
Clerk: Would you like it sent 'Greetings'?

JOB CENTRE

'What's the height requirement for the police force?'
'Five feet eight.'
'Damn, I'm an inch too tall.'

Foreman: Murphy, you phoned in sick yesterday but you were seen at the soccer match in the afternoon.
Murphy: No, not me. That was some feller who looked just like me. In fact, I told him so myself at half time.

BUILDING SITE

'Murphy, you're late!'
'I'm sorry, foreman, but my brother got burned.'
'Burned? How bad?'
'Well, they don't do things by halves at the crematorium.'

Murphy walked into a Dublin barber shop, asked for a Henry Winkler haircut like on the telly and fell asleep in the chair.

When he woke up, he discovered the barber had left him completely bald.

Fuming, Murphy yelled, 'You idiot, don't you know what Henry Winkler looks like?'

'Sure I do,' replied the barber. 'I watch him every week on Kojak.'

'Hello, Sally, are you working?'

'Not any more. I packed my last job in only yesterday. I just couldn't work with people looking at me.'

'What was your job?'

'Artist's model.'

SURGERY

'Doctor, can I have some more of those sleeping pills for my wife?'

'Why do you want some more?'

'She's woken up.'

Murphy's coat needed cleaning so he took it to a place that had a sign which read 'ONE DAY CLEANERS'. Returning there that afternoon, he was told his coat wasn't ready yet.

'But,' he protested, 'your sign says "ONE DAY CLEANERS".'

'That's true,' retorted the assistant, 'your jacket will be ready *one* day.'

DUBLIN PET SHOP

'I'd like to buy a tortoise.'

'Sorry. I had some delivered this morning but I've sold out. Tortoises go very quickly.'

'Funny, I always thought they went very slowly.'

Sign in the window of a Dublin barber shop on Saint Patrick's Day: All day today haircuts half price. Only one to a customer.

Irish cinema manager: Starting next week I'm going to shut my cinema on Sundays. Then, if it's a success, I'll shut it on weekdays too.'

DUBLIN BARBER SHOP

'Murphy, have you been neglecting your hair?'

'Indeed I have not. I take it with me everywhere I go!'

BUILDING SITE

Foreman: Hey, Murphy, how come you only carry one roof tile at a time and the other roofers carry thirty?

Murphy: Well, Boss, them other fellers are just too lazy to make more than one trip.

Irish palmist: 'When it comes to palms, I know 'em like the back of my hand.'

THE IRISH OUT AND ABOUT

Murphy saw a sign in the park which read: 'Refuse to be put in the litter bin.' Climbing into the bin, the contrary Murphy exclaimed. 'No one tells *me* what to do!'

Then there was the Irish rock 'n' roller who twisted his ankle doing the hand jive.

Then there was the Irish cowboy who only wore one spur. He reasoned that if the left side of the horse moves, the other side has to move too.

Shortsighted Irish mugger: Put your hands up! Well, are they up yet?

A Dublin cop saw a little boy standing in a shop doorway smoking a cigarette and taking swigs from a bottle of Guinness.

'Hey,' said the cop, 'why aren't you in school?'
Replied the kid, 'Because I'm only four years old!'

LOST PROPERTY OFFICE

'Has anyone handed in a pair of wellies?'
'What size?'
'Eleven. But I'll take a size twelve if that's the only pair you've got.'

After sampling the product from a Durex vending machine, Murphy confessed it was even chewier than Wrigley's, Orbit and Bubbleyum.

Irish bride to groom at the start of the honeymoon: Hurry up, I haven't got all night.

Irish Hell's Angels' motorbikes have training wheels.

Child molester: Hello, little girl, like to come for a ride in my car?
Irish kid: Okay, but only if you show me your willy.

SOHO

'Hey, do you want to buy some blue photos?'
'Let me see them first . . . Huh, you must take me for an idiot. These photos aren't blue, they're black and white!'

Two thieves broke into a Dublin electrical goods store.
'Hey, Mike,' said one, 'why don't you steal a TV set?'
'Oh, I couldn't do that,' replied his accomplice, 'I don't have a licence!'

Murphy got thrown out of a pub after he staggered into the bar and asked for a pint of Titbread's Wankard.

Murphy, visiting his first topless restaurant, studied a waitress' tiny boobs and surmised they were a child's portion.

Murphy walked into a pub carrying a parking meter so he'd remember where he parked his car.

ROMANTIC INTERLUDE

Murphy: Theresa, your dress is coming off!
Theresa: No, it's not!
Murphy: Yes, it is. I've made my mind up.

Murphy failed his driving test when he swerved to run over a cat.

POLICE INTERROGATION ROOM

'Murphy, where were you between eight and eleven last night?'
'Give me a clue!'

Murphy ran after a council water sprinkler to tell the driver his vehicle had sprung a leak.

WORLD WAR II

Sergeant: Look out, Clancy, there's a blazing bomber heading straight for us!
Clancy: No need to panic, Sarge, it's one of ours.

Ticket inspector: Ticket, please.
Passenger: My dog ate it.
Ticket inspector: Then you'd better buy him a second helping.

Irishman: I'm going to make love to you!
English woman: Well, if you do and I ever find out about it...

Then there was the Irish mystery coach tour. The passengers held a contest to guess their destination. The driver came fifth.

There's a town on the West coast of Ireland which is so dull that one day the tide went out and never came back.

Then there was the Irishman who told a Dublin fortune teller he wanted his palm read, so she painted it.

Then there was the Irishman who joined a fife band but quit when he ran out of bananas.

A Dublin jury acquitted a woman of murdering her husband because they felt sorry for her being a widow.

Then there was the Irishman who was arrested for urinating in a shop doorway late at night and charged with impersonating a police officer.

Then there was the Irish tramp who rang Mr Kipling's doorbell and begged for a slice of bread.

Murphy joined the church choir and 200 parishioners changed their religion.

DOCTOR'S WAITING ROOM

Patient: Have you 'flu?
Murphy: No, I came by bus.

Murphy, setting off for work, boarded a bus at the Town Hall. Glancing at the clock outside the building, he noticed it said 7.30. The bus's next stop was at a bank and he saw the clock in the window showed 7.15. 'Good grief,' exclaimed Murphy, 'I'm going in the wrong direction!'

Then there was the Irishman who went into Virgin Stores and tried to buy one.

An English kid and an Irish kid were arguing over which one could slide down the banisters the faster. The Irish kid claimed he could do it quicker even if he gave the English kid a head start. The English kid said that sounded fair to him, so he climbed on to the top of the banister and his Irish mate climbed on a few feet behind him. 'Oh, by the way,' exclaimed the English lad, 'no overtaking!'

'Doctor, I can't seem to get people to like me.'
'What gives you that impression?'
'Mind your own business.'

Murphy filled his mouth to capacity with cottage cheese and went to a fancy dress ball. 'And just what are you meant to be?' asked one of the judges. Punching himself in both cheeks simultaneously so the cheese shot all over the unfortunate man, Murphy replied, 'Acne!'

DUBLIN CAFE

'Waitress, this bowl of soup you served me – the bowl is filthy.'
'Oh no, sir, the bowl is clean. It's the soup that's dirty.'

There's such a backlog of cases to be tried in Dublin's courts that it's taking criminals longer to get into jail than it'll take 'em to get out.

Then there's the Irish Monks' Union who went on strike for worse conditions.

A poster outside a Dublin theatre has the slogan 'Book early to be sure of disappointment.'

'Have you got a *Catholic Herald* for a week back?'
'No. Have you tried sleeping on a wooden board?'

Did you know that Irish trains stop at level crossings to let cars go by?

I won't say Muldoon was a drunk but two weeks after he died his liver won a disco dancing contest.

Murphy won the pools and went on an ocean cruise in the Pacific. Spotting a pretty girl sunbathing by the ship's swimming pool, he walked over to her determined to chat her up. 'Hello there, darling,' was his opening line. 'Do you live around here?'

Murphy had his application for membership accepted by the local golf club. Told to bring his own caddy, he asked if he should empty the tea out first.

Sean and Tim are inseparable mates. Last Saturday night it took ten cops to separate them.

PALAIS

Girl: I have to be home by midnight.
Murphy: Well, I'm dancing as fast as I can.

Murphy's doctor told him he should take more exercise. So Murphy got rid of his car and bought a motor-cycle. instead.

DUBLIN MAGISTRATES COURT

'How do you plead? Guilty or not guilty?'
'Can I wait till I've heard the evidence before I make my mind up?'

Murphy is such a versatile sportsman that he suffers from pentathlete's foot.

Murphy is in hospital recovering from a bad case of whiskey.

Priest: On the day of judgement there will be weeping and wailing and gnashing of teeth.
Murphy: What if we don't have any teeth?
Priest: Teeth will be provided!

HAIRDRESSING SALON

'I'd like to buy a wig.'
'That's fifty pounds including tax.'
'Oh, never mind about the tacks. I'll glue it on!'

'Oh, Maureen, that furniture store salesman is a dirty devil.'

'What makes you say that, Molly?'

'Well, he offered me a free carpet as long as I had my underfelt!'

'Hi, Sean.'

'Hi, Tim. Haven't seen you for six months. What've you been doing?'

'Six months!'

INTRODUCTION

Murphy: Irish and proud of it.
Angus: Scotch and fond of it.

Murphy is such a useless driver, he has to stop the car so he can look down to see which is the brake.

Then there was the queer Irish boxer who was so worn out after each fight that he couldn't stay awake for two seconds.

Murphy admits he gets drunk after one whiskey. Usually the twenty-fifth.

DUBLIN SPORTS SHOP

'I'd like a shooting stick.'

'Anything else?'

'Yes, a box of bullets.'

53

In Irish funfairs, the wall of death motor bikes have seats for the disabled.

Driving home one hot summer afternoon, Murphy saw an exhausted toad in the middle of the road. Being a kind hearted soul, he stopped, got out, lifted the toad up and put it down in the shadow of his stationary car. Then, feeling very pleased with himself, he drove home.

Holidaying in Canada, the Murphys went to a Toronto taxidermist's and asked to see a mounted policeman.

Murphy was driving home one evening when he ran out of petrol. Fortunately, he'd stopped outside a filling station. Unfortunately, he'd left all his money behind and the attendant refused to let him have any petrol on tick. 'Fair enough,' shrugged Murphy, 'but tell me one thing, would I be doing the car any harm if I drove it home on an empty tank?'

There's a nightclub in Dublin which has an entrance fee of two pence. It's to keep the riff-raff out.

Did you hear about the Irish SAS man who stormed Dublin's Zoo, shot four gorillas and freed all the ostriches?

Then there's the one about the Irish brothel. It has bunk beds.

SLIMMING CLINIC

'Well, Mrs Kelly, have you done as I instructed two weeks ago and cut out potatoes?'

'Indeed I have. Of every one I cut out, I got six chips.'

Murphy spent so long at junior school that he had to play truant to get married.

When One-Eyed Riley gets drunk he sees single.

DUBLIN PUB

'Whiskey and soda?'

'Yes please . . . without the soda!'

Murphy paid £50 for a pullover. He was doing 95 on the motorway when a speed cop drove alongside and yelled, 'Pull over!'

SURGERY

'Mr Kelly, the last time you were here, I listened to your chest.'

'Oh yes? And what did it say about me?'

Traffic cop: What's your name?
Irishman: Greenhall.
Traffic cop: Where are you going?
Irishman: Southall.
Traffic cop: What make of car is this?
Irishman: Vauxhall.
Traffic cop: What've you got in the boot?
Irishman: Nothing.

Murphy visited wicked Soho and spent six hours outside a brothel waiting for the red light to turn green so he could go in.

MOVIE MEMORABILIA SHOP

'I want to buy Marilyn Monroe's autograph. Do you have it?'
'No, but I could do you one.'

Then there's the Irish strongman whose act consists of him tearing a telephone directory in half. Page by page.

Since passing his driving test, Murphy regularly takes his car out for a spin. Round lamp-posts.

Elections are held in Ireland just to test the accuracy of the opinion polls.

FAMILY DINING IN A RESTAURANT

Father: Oh, waiter, can I have a bag to take the leftovers home for the dog?
Little Boy: Whoopee! We're going to get a dog!

Murphy has alcoholic constipation. He hasn't passed a pub for ages.

The International Sprint Down Mount Everest Race was won by an Englishman. An Irishman was runner-up.

'Doctor, I've got a sore nose.'
'Well, stay off it till it gets better.'

Then there was the Irish bullfighter who started in a small way by waving a red hanky at an Oxo Cube.

Why are the Irish astronauts still on the Moon?
They forgot to buy *return* tickets.

An old lady with an ear trumpet walked into a Dublin library. The librarian approached and asked what it was she was holding. Replied the old girl, 'It's an ear trumpet!'
    'Well,' retorted the librarian, 'if I catch you playing it in here, out you go!'

'Phew, the weather is very close.'
'Then step back a few feet.'

Murphy lives in such a poor neighbourhood the dustmen don't collect, they deliver.

NON-SMOKING COMPARTMENT

Inspector: Whose is that cigarette on the floor?
Murphy: You can have it, you saw it first!

'Hey, Sean, would you like to buy a German car?'
'I would not. I can't speak the language.'

In aid of charity, a Dublin pub hired a famous entertainer to knock down a pile of drunks.

BETTING SHOP

'Hey, Sean, I just had a double come up.'
'A double?'
'Yes. Two non-runners.'

The Dublin Philharmonic Orchestra comprises fifty-five combs and papers and a musical saw.

How can you spot an optician's eye chart which was printed in Ireland?
The spelling has been corrected.

Murphy had his bike stolen in spite of taking safety precautions. Before leaving it, he distinctly remembers chaining the saddle to the crossbar.

'Hello there, Theresa. They tell me you've been to Rome for a holiday?'

'Indeed I have Molly. And I swear to God that those Italian men kept pinching my backside, so they did.'

'But *all* Italian men pinch girls' backsides.'

'Yes, but not with pliers.'

What's written on an Irish rainbow?
'Also available in other colours.'

RAILWAY STATION

'What time does the 7.45 train leave?'
'A quarter to eight.'

SURGERY

'Doctor, you know those kidney pills you gave me for my chest? Well, they're no good 'cos it's me back that's giving me the headaches.'

Murphy had just checked into the hospital for the first time in his life when the nurse asked him if he wanted a bedpan.

'What,' exclaimed Murphy. 'You mean I've got to do my own cooking?'

MAGISTRATES COURT

'How do you plead?'
'Not guilty.'
'Ever been in trouble with the police before?'
'No. Until now, I'd never stolen anything.'

POLICE INTERROGATION ROOM

Cop: Where were you at 9.30 last night, Miss Kelly?
Miss Kelly: I was taking a bath.
Cop: Any witnesses?

One-Eyed Riley stood at the front of a bus queue. When the bus arrived, he took out his glass eye, tossed it high into the air and caught it. When asked by the man behind him why he did such a thing, Riley replied, 'To see if there was any room on the top deck!'

The Irish Olympic Weightlifting event was cancelled because the starter lost his pistol.

Irish child molester: Hey little girl, would you like to go for a ride in a car? You would . . . ? Good . . . ! Do you *have* a car?

'Clancy, why did you and your wife turn down that invitation to my barbecue?'

'Because you're a snob! You think me and the missus aren't good enough to eat *inside* your house!'

Clancy had a terrible experience in hospital. He was being wheeled to the operating theatre to have his tonsils out when someone turned the trolley round.

What's a smart Irishman wear for ballroom dancing? Patent rubber wellies.

How can you spot upperclass Irish country ladies? They wear tweed donkey jackets and sensible wellies.

SURGERY

'Doctor, I'm losing my hair.'
'Don't worry, it'll all come out okay.'

As the hangman placed the noose around Finnegan's neck, the condemned man burst out laughing.

'And what's so funny?' queried the executioner.

'Just this!' laughed Finnegan. 'You're hanging the wrong man!'

'Is this Cockfosters?'
'No, it's mine!'

Then there was the short-sighted Irish tortoise that made love to an Army helmet.

Murphy: Excuse me, sir, but can you direct me to Camden High Street?
Turbanned sikh: Indeed, I can, my fine fellow. You turn left at the traffic lights.
Murphy: Thank you very much, sir and I hope your head soon gets better!

The doctor examined Murphy and exclaimed, 'Good God, man, you've got five penises. How on earth do your underpants fit?'
Replied Murphy, 'Like a glove.'

There's a photographic equipment shop in Dublin that's so narrow they don't have room to stock a wide angle lens.

Murphy has no kids because, as a schoolboy, he was teacher's pet and she had him doctored.

WAR

C.O.: Fire at will!
Murphy: Will who?

LA BELLE Y ACHE

Dublin's finest restaurant
(A five scar eating house as mentioned
in *The Good Riddance Guide*)

MENU

TABLE D'HOD

STARTERS

Soup du Jour 15p
Soup du Yesterjour 7½p
Soup du Tomorrowjour 25p
Cream of Thumb soup 5p
Campbell's cream of Tate soap £1 (confused? you won't be)
Alphabet soup in alphabetical order 45p
Paddy de Fois Grease 30p
Frogs legs £1 a foot
Frogs legs cooked in their wellies £2
Frogs wings £2
Frogs drumsticks £1-50
Potted shrimps £1
Snookered shrimps £1
Avocado £1 per pair or 50p per pear
Boiled egg 15p
Boiled egg sunny side up 20p

MAIN COURSE

Chicken chass yeagh! £3 (Please tell waiter if you want
    stuffing)
Spagghheti 50p
Spaghetti correctly spelled 75p
Chef's special £2
Chef's wife (not very special) £1
Chef's surprise (don't tell chef what it is) £3
Duck under glass £5
Duck under glass A la Windowlene £6

Duck under the table (your wife just walked in) £6
Pig's head £4
Pig's head English style (brains removed) 2p
T-bone £3
T-bone with steak £7
Wood pigeon £5
Metal pigeon £4
Mixed grill (Potatoes cooked 5 different ways) £2
Shishka Bog £3

VEGETABLES

New potatoes 50p
Secondhand potatoes 20p
Potatoes baked in their donkey jackets 65p
Green salad (lawn mower permitting) 60p
Cut green beans 40p
Half-cut green beans (cooked in Guinness) 60p
Horse Radish (subject to availability of horse) 45p
Thousand Island dressing 30p
Five Hundred Island dressing (half the calories) 15p
Catsup 20p
Catsdown 25p
Catsupsidedown 35p

CHEESE BOARD

English Cheddar 50p
Irish Cheddar (like English but thicker) £1
Swiss cheese 70p
Swiss cheese with holes 80p
Extra portion of holes 35p

BOOZE LIST

Champagne (per can) £1
Champagne (per cup) 12p
Scotch 30p
Irish Scotch 35p

Phyllosan 40p
Phyllosan (child's portion) 80p
Guinness (enough to get you pissed) £150
VAT 69 (including 69% VAT) 69p
Colt 45 45p
Any other year Colt 50p
Red wine £4
White wine £5
Red & white striped wine £9
Wine (your choice of colour) £8
Lager 60p
Lager with Lime (Lime by the shovelful) 65p
Clean glass 10p extra
Window seat £1 extra

AFTERS

Plums 25p
Plums which become Prunes because you wait so long 15p
Custard 5p
Custard (filleted) 7p
Ice cream a la mode 50p
Ice cream a la mode without mode 25p
Mode a la mode without ice cream free
Double portion of above 6p
Window seat *inside* restaurant £2 extra
Choice of tablecloth (*The Sun, Daily Mirror, The Times,* etc) 20p
Tablecloth (back issue) 10p
We are open 24 hours a day. Longer at weekends.
Credit cards: American Access, Carte Belche, Diners Clod, etc.
The optional service charge is compulsory.
All prices inclusive of cracked crockery.
Not licensed for singing or fighting. (Fighting license applied for.)
Customers who pay for their meal and sneak out without eating it will be prosecuted.

We do not serve children. Please bring your own.
Homosexual customers please use rear entrance.
Spittoons, Enemas, Stomach pumps courtesy of management.
If you feel your bill has been incorrectly multiplied, please ask to see the manager and give him the name of your next of kin.
Our staff do not solicit for gratuities because they don't know what it means.

'That Theresa Kelly over there has been aggravating me all evening.'

'But Theresa hasn't even looked at you.'

'I know, that's what's aggravating me!'

Murphy staggered out of the pub and into the nearest shop. Slumping down in the nearest chair he asked for a haircut.

'Okay,' retorted the barber, 'but take your hat off.'

'Why?' asked Murphy. 'Are there ladies present?'

Murphy went fly fishing and caught sixteen bluebottles.

Murphy grew up in a small village in Ireland and, although he had a TV set, he'd never been to a cinema. On holiday in Dublin he decided to remedy this and went to a nearby Odeon where he sat through an excellent western. As he left the cinema, the commissionaire asked him what he thought of it. 'My God,' exclaimed Murphy, 'the reception is superb!'

Sign in window of a Dublin restaurant: Man wanted to wash dishes and a waitress.

Murphy and eleven of his mates had a night out in a swank Dublin restaurant. They wined and dined well, and when the bill arrived Murphy took charge of dividing it into twelve equal amounts. He ticked off the twelve soups, the twelve main courses, the twelve desserts and the twelve bottles of wine, but then something on the bill caught his eye. 'Okay,' he snarled accusingly, 'which greedy swine ordered the Value Added Tax?'

Then there was the famous Irish explorer who died of starvation trying to find his mouth.

Murphy got off a charge of wife beating after his missus failed to pick him out in the police identity parade.

At the last Winter Olympics, the Irish Bobsled team refused to go down the Cresta Run until it was gritted.

Priest: Theresa, if you've led a pure life you can get married in a white dress. If you've led an impure life you should get married in a blue one.
Theresa: Would it be all right if I wore a dress with a blue and white check pattern?

Doctor: Murphy, you have schizophrenia!
Murphy: I don't believe you and neither do I!

CAFE

'Milk?'
'Please.'
'Sugar?'
'Please.'
'Slice of lemon?'
'Please.'
'Tea?'
'No thanks, hate it!'

I won't say Maureen is a dangerous motorist but she drives like she *owns* the pavement.

When Murphy walked into a topless restaurant, he was so embarrassed he didn't know where to look for the best.

VISITOR TO A FARMYARD

'Farmer, one of your hens has stopped laying.'
'How can you tell?'
'I just ran over it!'

TIM AND SEAN IN A BOAT

'Hey, Tim, we've sprung a leak! Start bailing!'
'No need to, Sean. The water will run over the sides when the boat gets full.'

Whore: Hello, sailor, what would you say to a little nookie?
Irish sailor: I'd say, 'Hello, little nookie'.

DUBLIN STREET AT NIGHT

Whore: Like a nice time?
Man: I've only got 10p.
Whore: That's okay, I've got change.

Motorway Cop: Okay, chummy, I'm nicking you for speeding.
Murphy: I wasn't speeding, officer. Mind you, I've just passed a dozen guys who were.

Murphy got drunk, walked into a grandfather clock and tried to make a phone call.

'Tell me, Sean, why did you move from the house next door to the church to the house next door to the brewery?'
'Well, Tim, the view may not be so good but the air is more intoxicating.'

DUBLIN LIBRARY

'Do you like Kipling?'
'I don't know, I've never been kippled.'

Murphy is a do-it-yourself fanatic. He put up the shed on his allotment. Eight times so far.

'You know, Sean, I'll never understand reggae.'
'What do you mean, Tim?'
'Well, by the time I've worked out what the tune is, they're playing something else.'

'Hey, Tim, how did you break your leg?'

'Oh, I saw a spider on the pub ceiling and tried to step on it.'

Did you hear about Ireland's first heart transplant? The recipient died in a car crash; the donor got better, so they gave him his heart back but his body rejected it.

'Excuse me, but can you tell me where the other side of the road is?'

'Yes, it's over there.'

'That's funny, a feller over there sent me over here.'

Murphy is so cheap that he switches off his windscreen wipers when he drives under a bridge.

Then there was the Irish soccer team who reached the semi-finals of the F.A. Cup. They said if they win they don't want any publicity.

Then there was the Irish cricket match which was abandoned because both teams showed up wearing white.

Winning £15 on the Derby, Murphy celebrated by splashing out on a new pair of boots. Then he had to wait till they were dry before he could go home.

Did you hear about the Irish nudist camp sports day? In the sack race all the competitors wore polythene bags.

Murphy's doctor examined him and advised him to take more exercise. 'Go to your local golf course and play thirty-six holes,' said the G.P. So, on the way to the golf course, Murphy bought himself a harmonica.

'Hey, Maureen, where did you meet your husband?'
'Oh, Molly, it was at the local dance. He was the handsomest feller on the floor. I can see him now . . . lying there.'

The Irish athletic team were disqualified from the Olympic Games when sex tests revealed that seven members of the men's team were found to be women.

After Evel Knievel jumped his motorbike across the Grand Canyon, the Irish tried it but all four members of their relay team were killed.

Murphy went to Scotland Yard and demanded to see the Flying Squad. Asked to state his reason, he admitted someone had stolen his kite.

Six feet four inch Sean went steady with three feet eleven inch Molly. Eventually he jacked it in.

Sign on front door of Dublin City Hall: *No admittance unless you want to come in.*

Attendances at Irish soccer matches are so bad that one newspaper is running a Spot the Spectator contest.

Irish package tour holiday: Fourteen days and three nights.

Then there was the Irish motorist in Birmingham who said to a pedestrian, 'Can you direct me to Spaghetti Junction? I'm starving.'

Mulrooney, who had two wooden legs, got struck by lightning and burned to the ground.

Murphy spends a lot in pubs. Not money – time.

DUBLIN CAR ACCESSORIES SHOP

'A twelve foot long starting handle, please.'
'What? A twelve foot one? Are you crazy?'
'No, I've got a Volkswagen and the engine's at the back.'

Then there was the Irish comedian who stole jokes from Bernard Manning.

Irish schoolboy: I know how to spell Mississippi but I never know when to stop.

Then there was the Irish criminal who hijacked the QE2 in mid-Atlantic and demanded one million pounds and a getaway car.

The most crowded building in Dublin is the Claustrophobia Hospital.

Where do the Irish go when they holiday abroad?
Ireland.

Sean and Tim were out walking in the country when Sean fell down a dried-up well. Tim yelled down at him, 'Hey, Sean, is it dark down there?'
Yelled back Sean, 'I don't know, I can't see a thing.'

Maureen was thrown out of Irish Weight Watchers for cheating. They caught her weighing herself on the scale by standing on tiptoe.

A beautician talked Maureen into having a mud pack to improve her appearance. So Maureen had the mud pack and sure enough it improved her appearance for three whole weeks. Then it slid off.

Then there was the Irishman who came third in a duel.

Murphy pleaded innocent to a charge of shoplifting from a bookstore because he only took a book of free verse.

VILLAGE STORE

'Do you sell sealing wax?'

'No, but I can sell you some floor wax. If you want to put it on the ceiling, use it upside down.'

Old Matty Muldoon sat on a park bench, a paperback book in his wrinkled hands and tears in his eyes.

'What are you crying for, Matty?' asked a passing friend.

'Oh, I'm reading *Lady Chatterley's Lover*,' replied Matty.

'But, *Lady Chatterley's Lover* isn't a sad book,' comforted his friend.

Retorted Matty, 'It is when you get to my age!'

Murphy the hijacker demanded £1 million in used 50p pieces with non-consecutive dates.

DUBLIN HOTEL ROOM

Voice outside door: I have a letter for you, sir.

Guest: Slip it under the door.

Voice: I can't, sir, it's on a tray.

Murphy fell into the Liffey and yelled, 'Help, help, I can't swim, I can't swim! Not only that, but my hands are in my pockets!'

Shouted a passer-by, 'Then why not take your hands *out* of your pockets?'

'What?' yelled Murphy. 'And let the water in?'

ROAD ACCIDENT

Traffic policeman: What happened?
Motorist: Well, to avoid a collision, I ran into that car there.

Murphy: You don't get many homos in Dublin.
Homo: I do! I get as many as I want!

SOCCER GAME

Referee: I'll spin the coin. Murphy, you call.
Murphy: Heads!
Referee: It's tails. You lose!
Murphy: Spin it again.
Referee: Okay. You call, Murphy.
Murphy: Heads!
Referee: It's tails. You lose again!
Murphy: Spin it just once more and make it best two out of three.

Murphy saw a sign in a hospital waiting room which read 'No Smoking allowed'. So Murphy smoked quietly.

Murphy's a born loser. He was once fined for contempt of court at a sheepdog trial.

SEAN, PAT AND TIM OUT WALKING

Sean: Hey, lads, there's an off-license. Let's go in and buy three bags of crisps.
Pat: But we can't afford three bags of crisps.
Tim: Then let's buy one bag and pay half each.

'Hey, Sean, have you trained that dog of yours?'
'Indeed I have, Tim. I only have to say "Attack" to him
and he has one.'

6   81

POLICE STATION

'Oh, Constable, I've just received an anonymous letter.'
'Really, Mrs Kelly? Who from?'

Doc: Do you have any scars?
Murphy: No, but I've got a couple of cigarettes.

Sign in window of electrical goods store: *Starts Friday.
Sale of reconditioned gas cookers. Can't last.*

Murphy decided to take up hitchhiking. On the first day
he left home early to avoid the traffic.

'Doctor, I've got a corn.'
'On which foot?'
'The foot on the left hand side.'

It was late one Saturday night when Murphy's car ground
to a halt. Piston broke. Just like Murphy.

THE WIT AND WISDOM OF
THE IRISH

First Irish teenage girl: Hey, Theresa, listen to this letter I've just written to my boyfriend.

'Dear Pat. I want you to know that since we started going steady, I've had affairs with your two brothers, your five uncles, your boss, your boss's three brothers, my boss, my boss's five brothers, twenty-eight men at my office, one hundred and fifty-two men at the dance hall and two hundred and sixty-six men I met during my holiday.'

There's just one thing, though, Theresa, how shall I sign it?

Second Irish girl: How about . . . 'Yours faithfully'?

'Hey, Sean, what would your parents say if they knew you were an orphan?'

'What's on at the cinema, Tim?'
' *"The Little Green Men Meet The Little Green Women"*.'
'Hmm, sounds like a monster movie.'

Murphy had a heart transplant and sent the donor a get well card.

Written on the bottom of an Irish staircase: 'Stand on the right.'

ROMANTIC INTERLUDE

'Tell me, Theresa, am I the first man to sleep with you?'
'You will be, Mike, if you doze off.'

Maureen: Wouldn't it have been a great day for female emancipation if the first man to land on the Moon had been a woman.

They say that Murphy is absent minded. Which makes sense because Murphy's mind is absent.

Farmer to milking hand: Grogan, that milk you got from the cows this morning should've been delivered weeks ago!

Motto of the Irish Navy: Above Us The Waves.

Did you hear about the Irish electric eel? It runs on gas!

Have you noticed that just enough things happen each day to fill your newspaper?

An Englishman, a Scotsman and an Irishman sat on the floor. The Irishman fell off.

Murphy is so fat that instead of elastic in his underpants he has Swishrail.

Winning entry in Irish Crossword Puzzle.

Murphy is so dumb, he thinks 'freedom of the press' means he has the right to put a crease in his trousers whenever he wants to.

Murphy met Anna Ford and said, 'Tell me, where do you newsreaders get all your ideas for the news?'

Do Irish beef butchers have dripping taps?

'Sean, why is that T-shirt you've got on soaking wet?'
'Because it says on the label "Wash 'n' wear".'

There are two kinds of Irishmen: Drunk and not yet.

Maureen is so thick, she needs a shopping list when she goes to the toilet.

Motto of Ireland's biggest trade union: A good week's work for a good day's money.

Sean: Why, Maureen, you're crying.
Maureen: Yes, I know. I saw the doctor today.
Sean: Oh yes? How is he?
Maureen: He's fine but *I've* got a terminal disease.
Sean: A terminal disease? Are you serious or joking?
Maureen: I'm serious.
Sean: Thank God because I hate jokes like that.
Maureen: The doctor said I don't have long to live.
Sean: How long?
Maureen: He gave me a year.
Sean: Don't you worry, Maureen, my brother-in-law is a barrister. He'll get it reduced to six months or a fine.

Murphy looked for Eamonn Andrews' phone number in the S-Z volume because he heard Eamonn's number was X-Directory.

'Hey, Tim, would you say you live in the past?'
'Oh, no! Mind you, I *used* to.'

Theresa had a terrific time on holiday in Rome. Someone told her 'si si' was Italian for 'no no'.

'Sean, I understand the police made a number of arrests of fellers they caught peeping through the windows of the nurses' hostel at night.'
'Yes, I read about it in the paper.'
'Oh yes? How many fellers were arrested?'
'About twenty-eight of us.'

The wife of Phil the pub pianist died. So, as a mark of respect, from then on he only played the black keys.

'Do you watch much TV, Sean?'
'Oh, I only watch two programmes, that's all.'
'Which two?'
' "Mork" and "Mindy".'

Then there was the Irishman who thought Peyton Place was a Birds Eye product.

'Hey, Sean, who are you working for these days?'
'Same old firm, Tim. The wife and ten kids.'

'Hey, Tim, did you know that Brighton has a topless beach?'
'Well, Sean, if they ever decide to put a roof on it, maybe we'll get jobs as hod carriers.'

Murphy thought a peach was a suede apple.

What's an Irish waterbed?
A bath tub.

POEM

Sol O'Mongrundy
Born on a Monday
Got drunk on Tuesday
Got drunk on Wednesday
Got drunk on Thursday
Got drunk on Friday
Died on Saturday
Inquest on Sunday
Verdict: Natural causes.

Murphy smoked so many dog ends that his lips got hard-pad.

'You know, Tim, I wish I could afford a car like yours.'
'So do I!'

In spite of what the Irish believe, farting is *not* contagious.

'Why are you looking so glum, Sean?'
'Ah, Tim, it's me missus. She's told me I can only have sex with her twice a week.'
'Count your blessings, Sean, she's cut the milkman off completely.'

'I'm sure Molly will love me all the more when we're man and wife. They tell me she's crazy about married men.'

'Murphy, don't you ever think about anything else but booze?'
'Yes, but I fight it.'

Ireland's top film of the year: *Sons of the Virgin Soldiers*.

'Tell me, Sean, do you like opera?'
'Indeed I do, Tim. Except for the singing.'

'What do you think of that Tony Blackburn?'
'Oh, I wouldn't criticise the feller. After all, I may be a virgin meself one day.'

Murphy was three-quarters of the way through writing his autobiography when he realised he wasn't mentioned in it.

Sean: Ooooh, my stomach aches something terrible.
Tim: Have you taken a Rennie?
Sean: Yes, but I don't think it was that!

Only in a Dublin chemist shop could you buy fertility pills in a childproof bottle.

An Irish scientist has come up with a hair dryer which works under water.

Then there's the Irish Polo mint. The hole is on the *outside*.

The entire membership of the Irish MENSA Society fell downstairs and broke his leg.

Definition of an Irish firing squad. Six riflemen all wearing blindfolds.

'Where were you born, Sean?'
'Kerry.'
'What part?'
'All of me!'

SECONDARY SCHOOL

'Mrs Murphy, I've decided your son should learn elocution.'
'About time too, headmaster. He's useless at changing light bulbs.'

'Sean, I'm having some trouble with this crossword. Can you give me a two-letter word ending in "o"?'
'No!'
'A fat lot of help you are!'

Murphy thinks he put one over on British Rail because he bought a return ticket and isn't going back.

'THAT'S HIS STAG NIGHT RUINED!'

Irish wedding superstition: It's unlucky for the groom if the bride sees him wearing her wedding dress.

'What answer gets you 50% in an Irish exam?'
'I don't know.'
'Correct!'

Murphy is really smart. He can tell the difference between a genuine £7 note and a counterfeit one.

Irish Bumper Sticker: *I've never heard of J.R.*

'You know, Maureen, I was once married to Murphy but the marriage was annulled for non-consummation.'
'What? You were married to Murphy? I had no idea!'
'Neither did Murphy!'

Then there was the Irishman who thought a Range Rover was a cowboy's dog.

Irish photographer: Say 'chalk'.

'I've got a terrible cold.'
'Why don't you take something for it?'
'Okay, make me an offer!'

Maureen returned a half-empty bottle of Harvey's Bristol
Cream, saying that no matter how hard she rubbed it in,
her bust stayed the same size.

Murphy wrote to Freepost to get one for his dog.

The Irish Noah's Ark sank when the two whales on board stampeded.

Murphy bought a piano stool and then took it to bits to try and find the keyboard.

'Hey, Sean, would you like to buy a parakeet?'
'I don't have room for both but how much is just one?'

Excerpt from an Irish cookbook: Take a potato, then another potato, then another and another and another . . .

Murphy joined a riding school. When it came to the bareback riding lesson, he stripped to the waist.

'Hey, Tim, do you go bowling?'
'Indeed I do. Every night.'
'Any luck?'
'Well, one night I win, the next night I lose, the next night I win and so on.'
'Then why don't you only go bowling every *other* night?'

Then there was the Irishman who thought Sissy Spacek was a gay Russian astronaut.

'Hey, Tim, do you believe in drinking whiskey to cure a cold?'

'Only as a first resort.'

'I just missed seeing a blacksmith make a complete horse today.'

'What do you mean?'

'Well, when I got there he was just finishing nailing the feet on!'

If all the Irish politicians were laid end to end, they'd have their feet in each others' mouths.

Why do so many Irishmen have their front teeth missing? So they can shovel in potatoes without opening their mouths.

Adam and Eve *must* have been Irish. They ate from the same apple.

Murphy is so dim, he thinks Shirley Temple is a synagogue.

The Irish have invented something which enables you to look through a brick wall. It's called a window.

Murphy has two entries in the *Guinness Book of Records*. Firstly, as the first man to receive a foot transplant. Secondly, as the first man with two left feet.

Murphy is such a loser, even when he talks to himself he never has the last word.

Non-smoker Murphy thinks Player's Weights are footballers' testicles.

Murphy: I've just won the pools and I want you to design a house for me with two staircases.
Architect: Why *two* staircases?
Murphy: One for going up and the other for coming down.

NEWS FLASH

A gang have kidnapped the Nolan Sisters. They say that unless they get £10,000 they'll let them go.

Irish cocktail: Perrier and Water.

'You know, Sean, I must get my nails cut. Every time I pick my nose I knock my hat off!'

'Sean, I hear your wife's given birth to a son?'
'Indeed she has, and he's a boy.'
'What are you going to call him?'
'Buzby.'
'Buzby? Why Buzby?'
'Well, his crying keeps ringing in my ears.'

Murphy thought a sundial was a new GPO service he could ring to be sure of getting a good day for a picnic.

Murphy took out an accident insurance policy with Lloyds of Dublin. Some time later he had an accident at work which resulted in him losing both arms. The insurance claims adjuster arrived, studied Murphy's policy and announced the firm would pay for his sleeves to be shortened.

Murphy came to England, applied for Social Security and was given a form to fill in. In the space marked 'Sign here', he wrote 'Capricorn'.

Murphy claims that two-thirds of the world don't know how the other half lives.

'Tell me, Maureen, do you ever go out after dark?'
'Only at night time.'

Murphy is so useless, he can't even do wrong right.

'Tell me, Sean, were your forefathers Irish?'
'I didn't have four fathers, Tim. My mother narrowed it down to just two possibles.'

Murphy thinks 'local anaesthetic' means getting knocked out in your favourite pub.

'Hey, Sean, are you henpecked?'
'I am not! I know because my wife told me.'

'You know, Tim, my father's a sexagenarian.'
'Well, for a man of his age, it's disgusting.'

Irish mosquito nets have huge holes so that even enormous mosquitos can't get in.

'Oh, Mrs Shannon, I understand your daughter's given birth to a baby?'
'She has that, Mrs Kelly.'
'And just two months after her wedding, Mrs Shannon?'
'Ah well, Mrs Kelly, the poor girl's so innocent, she didn't realise how long she had to be pregnant.'

'Hey, Sean, why are you wearing a bandage on your foot? Is it injured?'
'Oh no, my other foot is the injured one.'
'Then why not wear the bandage on the other foot?'
'Because the bandaged one is injured worse.'

Murphy is always soberly dressed. He has black coffee stains all down his donkey jacket.

'You know, Tim, I hate fellers like Kelly. He's the type to pat you on the back to your face and then punch you on the nose behind your back!'

Murphy is such a hypochondriac, when he dies he wants to be buried next to a doctor.

'I've just swallowed a spider.'
'Then take something for it.'
'Not likely. Let it starve!'

Murphy is so out of shape that he gets exhausted riding escalators.

Murphy thinks the Fleet Air Arm is where a sailor squirts his deodorant.

Murphy finds sex so satisfying that he can't wait to try it with another person.

Murphy is so stupid, he goes to orgies just for the grapes.

How can you identify an Irish obscene caller?
Heavy belching.

PHONE CALL

'Is that Dublin 1212?'

'No, it's Dublin 1213.'

'Well, can you pop next door and tell them they're wanted on the phone?'

Small ad in Dublin paper: Man wishes to sell hardly used camera and 20 photos of his right eye.

Murphy broke his leg and the doctor put it in a cast, telling Murphy that on no account should he climb stairs until the leg had healed and the cast had been removed. When X-rays showed the leg had mended, Murphy asked if he could now climb stairs. 'Certainly,' replied the doctor.

'Thank God for that,' retorted Murphy. 'I'm sick of shinning up and down that drainpipe every night to reach the bedroom!'

Sean: Maureen, I've been thinking. What'll happen to you when I'm dead?

Maureen: Well, with any luck, I'll be acquitted.

Murphy got hold of a phone directory and started to read it. Impatient to discover how it ended, he turned to the last page and exclaimed, 'Glory be! Zuckerman did it!'

JOB CENTRE

Interviewer: How long were you with your last employer?

Applicant: Thirty-five years.

Interviewer: Thirty-five years? How old are you?

Applicant: Twenty-eight.
Interviewer: Well, if you're only twenty-eight, how could you have worked for thirty-five years?
Applicant: Overtime.

Motto of the Irish Archaeological Society: Let bygones be bygones.

An Irish sparrow builds its nest with a hole at the bottom. It likes laying eggs but doesn't want to raise a family.

Murphy wrote to the Irish Water Board demanding a rebate, so they sent him back 100 gallons.

Murphy: Sure I know Mulligan but I'm not one of his closest friends. But then neither are his closest friends.

Irish proverb: A bird in the hand is a damn nuisance when you pick your nose.

Murphy says that the new British Rail Intercity Express trains enable passengers to arrive late much faster.

ROMANTIC INTERLUDE

'Tell me, Molly, am I the only man you've ever kissed?'
'Indeed you are, Pat, but not the best looking.'

O'Bannion is ninety-eight and he's never had a sick day in his life. Mind you, he's had a hell of a lot of sick nights.

When Charlie Chaplin's corpse was stolen, the Irish Charlie Chaplin Appreciation Society offered a £10,000 reward for its recovery . . . dead or alive.

'Hey, Murphy, what's Pat's last name?'
'Pat who?'

'I'm a loving family man, Tim, but I'd give me ten kids just to get rid of that wife of mine!'

'Hey, Murphy, who gave you those two black eyes?'
'No one gave me two black eyes, Tim. I had to fight for 'em.'

Then there's the Irish gynaecologist who really wanted to be a brain surgeon but he wasn't tall enough.

Murphy grew a moustache to hide his weak chin.

Then there was the Irishman who bought a pork pie hat but it went mouldy.

Then there was the Irishman who thought the Victoria Line was 'We are not amused'.

Murphy thought Lita Roza was a bottle of Italian red wine.

Did you hear about the Irish prostitute who divorced her husband for being unfaithful?

'Hey, Sean, would you like to buy these wellies I'm wearing?'
'No thanks, Tim.'
'Then I'll give you a quid to take 'em off my hands.'

Murphy's memorised over 2,000 phone numbers. Unfortunately he hasn't memorised the names to go with them.

Did you hear about the Irish incinerator?
It's made of plastic.

Then there's the Irish tricycle.
It has four wheels.

Then there was the Irishman who thought Little Red Riding Hood was a Russian condom.

Jewish Dubliner: I'm getting fed up with motzah balls. Isn't there some other part of a motzah worth eating?

Murphy got his missus to sew pockets in his skin so he'd have somewhere to put his hands when he was naked.

Molly has everything a man could wish for. Moustache, muscles and a hairy chest.

Excerpt from Irish Society Gossip Column: 'Theresa Ina Thomasina Shannon wore a dress cut so low in front that it revealed her initials.'

Two Irishmen were arguing over which was the bigger liar. Said one, 'I bobsleighed up Mount Everest.' Retorted his friend, 'I saw you.'

Murphy trained his parrot to say, 'Parrots can't talk.'

Irish film censor: I'm not against films which show rape, incest, bestiality and necrophilia, as long as they're done in good taste.

Murphy's horse tripped over his shotgun and accidently shot itself. So Murphy was forced to break its leg.

Tim: Oh, Molly, Molly, have you ever experienced the love that only happens once in a lifetime?
Molly: Oh, indeed I have, Tim. Hundreds of times.

Maureen gave up having egg shampoos because the chicken kept falling off her head.

Schizophrenia is a big problem in Ireland. Two in one people have it.

Murphy is so accident prone – not only to himself but to all he comes into contact with – that he has third party life insurance.

Irish scientists have invented a Vatican-approved birth pill. Women take one a night and it gives them a headache.

Murphy says he won't stop smoking 100 cigarettes a day because coughing is the only exercise he gets.

Then there was the Irishman who thought the Isle of Man T.T. Race was for motor bikes which run on milk.

Priest: Murphy, did you know that Adam and Eve started the human race?
Murphy: No. Who won?

'You know, Sean, that Gene Kelly feller is an idiot.'
'What makes you say that?'
'Well, he doesn't know enough to come in out of the rain.'

It's not that Murphy is a slow reader but he needs a bookmark to keep his place if he's interrupted reading a 'Stop' sign.

Young Billy Kelly and his grandfather both died on the same day. Grandfather died of old age and Billy died of *lack* of old age.

'Hey, Tim, Sean called me a selfish, ungrateful swine. And after all I've done to him.'

Then there's the Irish author who got the plot for his new novel from the movie version of his last novel.

'You know, Sean, old songs are the best songs.'
'Indeed they are, Tim. A pity they don't write old songs anymore.'

'Doctor, this low-calorie diet you've put me on, do I eat it before or after meals?'

If ignorance is bliss, why do the Irish always look so miserable?

An Irish scientist invented an acid so powerful it will dissolve anything. Unfortunately, he can't find a container to keep it in.

Never trust a hypnotist who won't look you in the eye.

Cop: Murphy, I've had a complaint that your dog has been chasing an old lady on a bike.
Murphy: That's rubbish, officer. My dog can't ride a bike.

Irish disc jockey: And now, 'Somewhere My Love Lies Sleeping' with the Ray Conniff Singers.

'You know, Sean, I'm so depressed I think I'll kill myself.'
'Oh don't, Tim, you'll only live to regret it.'

Definition of a belch.
Irish mating call.

Murphy thought bifocals were what you wore to look at David Bowie.

'How's the weather, Sean?'
'Pissing like a newt!'

Isn't it clever how the alphabet is in alphabetical order?

Then there's the Irishman who thinks a yashmak is what you wear when it rains yash.

Murphy is dextriambrous. He's unable to write with either hand.

The new Irish deodorant comes in a twinpack. That's one for each nostril.

Molly: Tell me, Mrs Kelly, was your husband's funeral expensive?
Widow: Well, for the past six years it's cost me £50 a week.
Molly: Fifty pounds a week?
Widow: Indeed yes. I buried him in a Moss Bros. rented suit.

What do you call an Irishman who's been banned from his local pub?
Homesick.

Christmas has become so popular in Ireland that the Government are to make it an annual event.

'Hey, Theresa, let's go somewhere where we can be alone.'

'Okay, Tim, and afterwards we'll meet back here.'

'Sean, why do they always have Christmas in December when the stores are so crowded?'

'Mrs Kelly, I understand your son is asexual.'

'That's as maybe, but I've never been able to catch him at it.'

Murphy saw a sign outside a factory which read THOMPSON'S TOOL WORKS. Said Murphy, 'So does mine but I don't brag about it.'

Then there was the Irish couple who tried unsuccessfully for fifteen years to have a baby in spite of both women taking fertility pills.

Credit cards have proved you don't have to be rich to be rich.

Muldoon is so old that his blood group is obsolete.

'Are you married?'
'No, I'm a widow.'
'A widow?'
'Sure. If you don't believe me, ask my late husband.'

Sean: How many A-levels have you?
Tim: Twelve.
Sean: Are you sure?
Tim: I'm positive.
Sean: Only fools are positive.
Tim: Are you sure?
Sean: I'm positive.

Father O'Field wears second-hand dog collars which he buys from charity pet shops.

Ireland's National Day: Half W'it Monday.

Then there was the Irishman who thought a bigamist was a thick fog in Italy.

Did you hear about the Irish scientist who is working on a cure for wheatgerm?

'Hey, Tim, did you hear Des O'Connor's last record?'
'I hope so.'

An Irish cuckoo lays other birds' eggs in its own nest.

Then there was the Irishman who thought he'd been given counterfeit money in his change because two of his coins had the same date.

'You know, Pat, that Murphy is a useless feller.'
'He is that. He's as much use as a one-legged man in an arse kicking contest.'

Then there was the Irishman who couldn't afford to buy a TV set so he drilled a spyhole in his radio.

Small ad: Lost. Black wallet containing £100. Reward of £200 offered to finder.

Then there was the Irishman who thought a '57 Chevrolet was a flavour of Heinz soup.

What's an Irishman's favourite drink?
The next one.

'What's so great about Shakespeare's plays, Sean? They're just a lot of famous quotations strung together.'

On the Irish version of the TV show *Sale of the Century*, the quiz master's catchphrase is 'No Conferring'.

Then there's the Irish singer whose voice is so bad, even deaf people wouldn't read his lips.

Irish woman: Oh, Mrs Kelly, are you having a baby?
Pregnant Irish woman: Glory be, no, Mrs Mulligan. I'm carrying this for a friend.

Written on Irish potato: *Peel other end first.*

Murphy can't understand why his birthday suit only has one button.

Never tell an Irishman who's tight to hang loose.

Did you hear about the Irish Adam and Eve? Their children were adopted.

Tip for gardeners. Never use a garden sprinkler when it's raining or it'll get rusty.

Then there's the Irish Cinderella. As the clock struck midnight she lost her glass eye.

Why did the Irish chicken cross the road?
To ask Colonel Sanders for political asylum.

Irish hit tune: The Walk of the Bumble Bee.

Murphy thought a tomtit was a cat's falsie.

An Irish scientist crossed a parrot with a laughing hyena and got an animal that tells itself jokes and laughs. But not in that order.

Best selling Irish book: *Saint Patrick. An unauthorised autobiography.*

'Knock knock.'
'Who's there?'
'An Irish SAS man. Can you open the door, please?'

How can you spot an Irish motor car?
The boot at the back is a wellington.

Murphy bought a Skye terrier from a pet shop but took it back because it couldn't fly.

QUESTIONS & ANSWERS

Q: What do Siamese twins have that most people don't?
A: Quadrophonic sound.

Q: Who stood outside the Black Hole of Calcutta and starved to death?
A: Fifty Irish ticket touts.

Q: Where do Irish explorers wear snow shoes?
A: On their hands.

Q: What do you get if you catch mumps?
A: A penny a tail.

Q: What's unusual about a limpet mine?
A: The pit ponies have to swim.

Q: What's Polyfilla?
A: The insides of a parrot.

Q: Who was Joan of Arc?
A: Noah's wife.

Q: What's hydrophobia?
A: Fear of heights.

Q: What's the Irish sewage problem?
A: They've lost the formula.

Q: What's the average contents of a box of Irish matches?
A: Bubblegum.

Q: Who drew a gun on Jesse James?
A: A very fast Irish tattooist.

Q: What's the first word in the shorter Irish Dictionary?
A: Zebra.

Q: What's a Hindu?
A: Lays eggs.

Q: What's Urdu?
A: What an Urdresser gives you.

Q: Who was St Ivel?
A: He built the Ivel Tower.

Q: How does an Irishman learn the piano?
A: One word at a time.

Q: What colour is a donkey jacket?
A: Navvy blue.

Q: What's a suffragette?
A: Someone who lives in the flypath of Shannon Airport.

Q: What are kilohertz?
A: Sadistic hit men.

Q: What do you know about Elke Sommer?
A: It's the Canadian moose hunting season.

Q: What's a casbah?
A: A place where you can get a pint of cas.

Q: Who said 'an eye for an eye and a tooth for a tooth'?
A: Dr Christian Barnard.

Q: Who was married to Ben Lyon?
A: Mrs Ben Lyoness.

Q: What's a tallboy?
A: The tallest member of the Walton family.

Q: What's a paddyfield?
A: An allotment where they grow Irishmen.

Q: Explain 'apéritif'.
A: It's a set of dentures.

Q: Who's the leader of Ireland's Moslems?
A: The Eiretollah.

Q: Who was Saint Michael?
A: Patron Saint of Underwear.

Q: Why does an Irish homing pigeon take ten times as long to reach its destination as an English homing pigeon?
A: Because the sender ties the message to its *wing*.

Q: How can you spot an Irishman in London on a Saturday night?
A: He's between two policemen.

Q: What's a somnambupist?
A: An Irish drunk who goes sleep-staggering.

Q: What's a sign of a gifted Irish child?
A: He goes from playschool to playuniversity.

Q: Who is Lord of the Flies?
A: Mr Wrangler.

Q: What is Scotch broth?
A: Irish stew and whiskey.

Q. Whose slogan is 'Don't cheat on the cheese'?
A: The Society of Irish Chiropodists.

IRISH INVENTIONS

Air-conditioned Pogo Stick

Solar-powered Nightlight

An Out-patient Morgue

Bullet-proof Target

Digital Floral Clock

Deepsea Divers Raindance Suit

Spanish Fly Swatter

Inflatable Voodoo Doll

A Mind Deboggler (for when your mind boggles)

Left Handed Octopus

A Fertility Condom

Free Range Easter Eggs

A Crockery Tumble Dryer

Counterfeit Toilet Paper

A Reverse Charge Ransom Note

Remote Controlled Hand Warmer

Arthritic Copper Handcuffs

Waterproof Sandals

A Designer Donkey Jacket

Contract lenses (for reading the small print in contracts)

A Mental Arithmetic Pocket Calculator

Funeral Confetti

A Discount Post Office

Radio With Subtitles For The Deaf

Skinless Onions

A Cuckoo Stopwatch

Unwrapped Sliced Bread

Chauffeur Driven Unicycle

Maternity Skis

Fatcea Bread

Internal Car Bumpers

A Bifocal Blindfold

An Alarm Sundial

A Teflon Magnet

Cut-throat Electric Razor

Portable Le Mans Racetrack

Disposable Eternity Rings

Battery Operated Power Station

Citizens Band Semaphore

Silicon Mash

A Steam Powered Kettle

Ping (deodorised ping-pong)

Petrol Pump Pilot Light

Individually Wrapped Salt

Steel Wool For Darning

A Home For Homeless Homos

Frozen TV Dinner Gong

Garbage Preserver

Wheelbarrow Grand National

Croissant Poultice

Suppository Snuff

A Knuckle Duster Duster

Handgrenade In A Ring Pull Can

Lumbar Puncture Repair Outfit

X-Directory Megaphone

Weed Fertiliser

Shroud Hand-me-downs

Stock Wheelchair Racing

Filleted Herringbone Jacket

Invisible Ink Tattoos

A Bowie Fork

Geriatric Maternity Ward

Styptic Typewriter

Self-raising Hat

Goldfish Dry Cleaner

A Code Of The West Decoder

Reversible Romper Suits For Backward Children

Colander Fart Remover

Elastic Seat Belt

A One-size-fits-all Birthday Suit

A Water Hammock

An Eye-level Urinal

Nair Restorer

Soya Mints

Concorde Roof Luggage Rack

Boil-in-the-bag Ice Cubes

A Kick-start Egg Timer

Tag Shadow Boxing

An Attache Carrier Bag

Divining Rod For Sailors On Submarines

HUMOUR

0352300698	**WOODY ALLEN** **Getting Even**	£1.00*
0352398973	**ALIDA BAXTER** **Flat On My Back**	75p
0352397187	**Out On My Ear**	75p
0352397101	**Up To My Neck**	75p
0352303565	**Upside-Down Under**	85p
0352301988	**Don't Hang Up,** **Sophie—It's God**	60p
0352304049	**GARRY CHAMBERS** **The (Almost) Complete** **Irish Gag Book**	70p
0352306408	**The Second (Almost)** **Complete Irish Gag Book**	85p

THE TWO RONNIES
EDITED BY PETER VINCENT AND IAN DAVIDSON

035230796X	**The Two Ronnies: And It's** **Hello From Him**	£1.00
035239899X	**The Two Ronnies: But First** **The News**	75p
0352301082	**More of the Two Ronnies:** **Nice To Be With You** **Again**	75p
0352302046	**The Two Ronnies:** **In A Packed Programme** **Tonight**	75p
0352302496	**The Bumper Book of The** **Two Ronnies**	75p
0352303123	**The Two Ronnies'** **Sketchbook** **(Large Format Illus.)**	£1.50
0352304278	**SPIKE MULLINS** **Ronnie in The Chair**	75p

* Not for sale in Canada. ● Reissues.
△ Film & T.V. tie-ins.

HUMOUR

	PATRICK CAMPBELL	
0352305290	A Feast of True Fandangles	£1.25
0352303662	My Life and Easy Times	95p
	DAVID DAWSON	
0352302097	Vet in The Vale	60p
0352301848	Vet in The Paddock	60p
	LES DAWSON	
0352304316	The Cosmo Smallpiece Guide to Male Liberation	75p
	ALEX DUNCAN	
0352398612	It's A Vet's Life	75p
0352398795	The Vet Has Nine Lives	75p
0352395389	Vets in Congress	75p
0352395699	Vet Among The Pigeons	75p
0352397020	Vets in the Belfry	75p
0352302186	Vet's Choice	70p
035230250X	Vet in the Manger	75p
035230328X	Vet in a State	70p
0352303573	Vet on Vacation	75p
	ERNEST EISLER	
0427004462	There Was A Young Lady (illus)	£2.50
	GORDON IRVING & IAN HEATH	
0352306890	Take No Notice	£1.00
	DERMOT KENNEDY	
0352305339	Panic in the Pulpit	95p
0352303433	Stumbling in the Aisles	75p
	IAN MESSITER & WILLIAM RUSHTON	
035230555X	The Impossible Quiz Book	95p

* Not for sale in Canada. ● Reissues.
Δ Film & T.V. tie-ins

Wyndham Books are obtainable from many booksellers and newsagents. If you have any difficulty please send purchase price plus postage on the scale below to:

Wyndham Cash Sales
P.O. Box 11
Falmouth
Cornwall
OR
Star Book Service,
G.P.O. Box 29,
Douglas,
Isle of Man,
British Isles.

While every effort is made to keep prices low, it is sometimes necessary to increase prices at short notice. Wyndham Books reserve the right to show new retail prices on covers which may differ from those advertised in the text or elsewhere.

Postage and Packing Rate

UK: 40p for the first book, 18p for the second book and 13p for each additional book ordered to a maximum charge of £1.49p.
BFPO and EIRE: 40p for the first book, 18p for the second book, 13p per copy for the next 7 books, thereafter 7p per book.
Overseas: 60p for the first book and 18p per copy for each additional book.